A NICE PLACE TO LIVE

(4 STORIES)

Paul Perilli

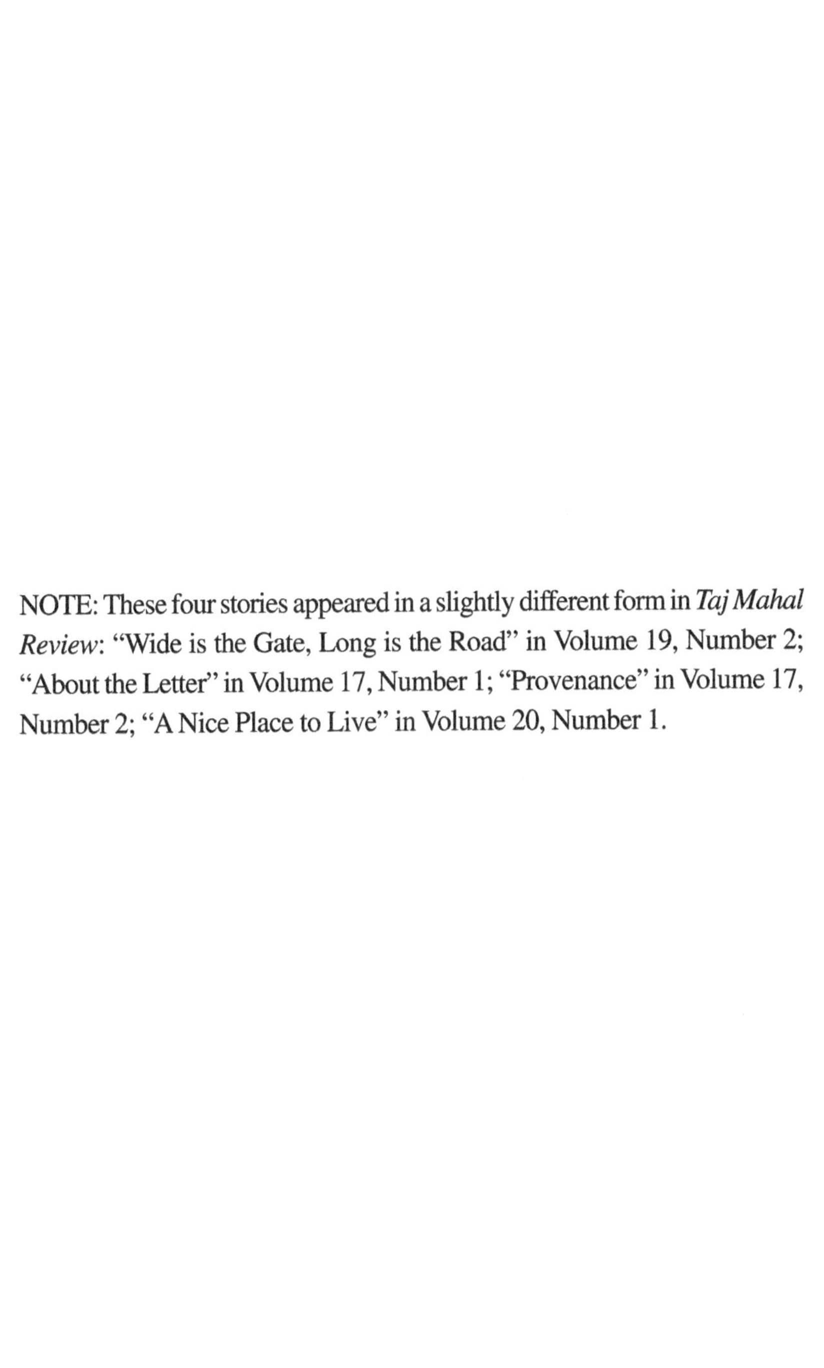

NOTE: These four stories appeared in a slightly different form in *Taj Mahal Review*: "Wide is the Gate, Long is the Road" in Volume 19, Number 2; "About the Letter" in Volume 17, Number 1; "Provenance" in Volume 17, Number 2; "A Nice Place to Live" in Volume 20, Number 1.

Contents

WIDE IS THE GATE, LONG IS THE ROAD

John Rossi and Ed Davis go in the door of Brewery Lane where Francis Martin, a tall, tattooed man in his thirties stands at the row of taps pouring a pint. He holds the glass upright with one hand and flips the handle back with the other to finish it off. Satisfied with the foamy head, he hands it to the customer and steps to the register.

His name is Francis Martin but Rossi and Davis have called him Father Francis since they started meeting at Brewery Lane on Sunday evenings, as if it's a place of worship they're intending to pray in. Though instead of a nave and transept, the former carriage house is a big open space stripped to its beams and brick. Instead of an altar, its main attraction is the chalkboard with a list of beers that Rossi and Davis check out.

Francis Martin is back shaking their hands, and says, "Got some good stuff for you."

"That's why we keep coming here," Rossi says.

Knowing their preferences, Francis Martin describes several, preaching to the choir, as they are, about what's hoppy and what *he* likes the most. In the time it takes them to decide, and as the urge strikes him, Francis Martin fills a goblet, gives it a sniff and throws it back in two giant gulps.

That, in fact, is another joke about him Rossi and Davis tell themselves, though they're too far removed from the antics of their younger days to think it's funny: Francis Martin drinks one for every five he pours. His Sunday night partner Eric knows this better than anyone.

Francis Martin uses two fingers to dry his lips. "So what's it going to be boys? A couple of IPAs?"

They wait as Francis Martin pours them one at a time. He takes their cash cards and they step past the walk-in refrigerator to a small, wobbly table next to the wood stove in back, where the smell of smoke, hops and damp is strong. The smell of a dive bar even if this one is for craft beer worshippers willing to cough up eight to twelve bucks a pint.

Rossi jerks his head out. "He knocked that one off like it was water to a thirsty man."

"I don't know how he does it. He's drinking more instead of less. All the sampling to make sure he knows what he's selling us. It's an important public service he's taken to the extreme."

"I'd say it's a good way to relax after some art making, but we know it ain't that at all."

Earlier in the year Francis Martin, the artist Francis Martin, had three paintings in a group show in a university gallery out on Long Island. He gave Rossi and Davis printed invitations and the following Friday night they drove to it from Brooklyn in Rossi's car.

Holding cups of red wine, Francis Martin stood with them as they looked over his three abstract portraits crafted with expressive brushstrokes that distorted the subject's features so the emotional impact was disconcerting. Francis Martin told them how he decided painting was what he wanted to do with his life after he got hold of a book about Pierre Bonnard. He was eighteen and attracted to Bonnard's figures and urban scenes of Paris. He'd painted traditional watercolors before that, but Bonnard released him from some inner restraint he'd put on himself up to then. After that, he shook their hands and moved on to talk to others.

"This is a side of him I would have never believed if I didn't see it," Rossi said.

They were impressed with Francis Martin's paintings. With the contrast between the soft colors and physical alterations. On the drive back they declared him a virtuoso.

"I didn't know what to expect, but it wasn't what I saw," Davis said.

A month later Rossi visited Francis Martin's one-bedroom apartment on a rundown block near the Montrose Ave. subway station. It also functioned as his studio. Or was it a studio that also functioned as a living space?

"There's not much living going on as we traditionally think of it," Rossi told Davis the next time they met up in Brewery Lane. "It's a place to paint and crash. But man, like we talked about, his stuff is strange and good. He told me he wakes up at night, does some work, then he goes back to sleep. Some nights he does that two or three times. I don't think he ever relaxes."

Davis touched a finger to his forehead to suggest he was seeing back into that moment. "You had a few pops, I presume."

"I brought burritos. Father Francis supplied the refreshments. We drained a growler and a couple of cans. High test stuff. Eight percent. He claims it gives him clarity. Helps him go deeper into his subjects. I had a headache in the morning. He must always have one. We didn't talk about this?"

"Not really, but now I understand how he loosened six hundred bucks from your wallet."

"I expected to buy something, but not to spend that much. He offered me a twofer discount at the friend's rate. What could I do? So I made a run to the cash machine. The brews had something to do with it."

From there Rossi told Davis everything else they talked about on his visit. How Francis Martin grew up in half a dozen small eastern Colorado towns. How he and his three siblings were raised by a single mother who liked alcohol more than she liked being a mother. How one of her favorite sayings was "Wide is the gate and long is the road that leads to destruction so many can't avoid." Francis Martin never knew where she got that from. She wasn't a churchgoer. As far as he knew she never read the *Bible*. But every so often she'd repeat it and he continued to wonder if it was a warning to her children or herself? However it was meant, she didn't follow her own advice. Her children didn't listen to it either.

Francis Martin was twenty when he left a job as a shipper-receiver at the Safeway in a town of seven thousand to move to Denver to take art classes. He couldn't stand small town life anymore. If he wanted to be an artist, he had to get away from that whole dreadful situation.

He found restaurant work and rented rooms here and there. In a few years he moved on to bartending and he'd supported himself in the business ever since.

"And here he is, through the gate and on the long road," Rossi said in summary.

The next Sunday they're back at the table by the wood stove when Francis Martin stops by to have a chat. His words come fast, and too loud for regular conversation. It's obvious he's been testing the product.

"You boys can't get enough of the smoke back here, even when a table's open up front. Don't you get that's why it's always free? No one wants to sit here unless there's no other option." Francis Martin smiles.

"I'm not fearing getting black lung, just yet," Rossi says.

"We'd have to spend a lot more time here than we do," Davis says. "I'm not saying that would be a bad thing."

"Next round's on the house," Francis Martin says.

"That means we're drinking at least one more," Rossi says.

Francis Martin collects the empty glasses off the tables. He's back at the taps a few minutes when a commotion starts up that Rossi interprets as two voices in a disagreement. One of those voices is Francis

Martin's. The other is a thick-bodied man standing with two others. It's not the first time they've seen Francis Martin get into it with a customer.

"That is so dumb." Francis Martin's words overpower its opposition. By then most everyone's looking that way. "Why don't you want to drink that? I told you what it was. Now you take a sip and give it back to me. I just can't waste beer on people who don't know what they like."

"I don't see how you stay in business, talking this way to your customers."

"I only do it to the ones who don't know what they want but order anyway. You ask for it, you pay for it. That's it."

"It's not like you described." The man looks to Eric, who continues to stay out of it.

"It's *exactly* how I described."

The man turns away from Francis Martin. When he turns back, he says, "Have it your way." He fingers a few bills from his wallet and gives them up to Francis Martin. He and his companions are at the door when Francis Martin says, "Don't come back when I'm working."

"You can be sure of it," is the response before the door clicks closed.

At the taps a while later, Francis Martin is still fuming. His eyes are tight and cheeks red. "People fucking piss me off. He wants a sour beer, so I give him a sour beer. One sip, he tells me it isn't what he thought. It's a sour. You don't know what sour tastes like? He wants something else. He doesn't want to pay for the sour."

"I get it," Rossi says. "Sours aren't for everyone. But once it's poured, you can't take it back."

"You got that right." Francis Martin rubs his hands together and picks a pint glass off the shelf. "This one's on me. What'll it be?"

The next Sunday Eric's there as usual, only he has a new partner, a woman he introduces as Rosemary. Right away it's obvious she has a softer outlook on things than Francis Martin.

"How has your day been going so far?" she asks them.

They're by the board getting ready to order. Eric crosses his arms and confirms what they know. "The boss caught wind of what happened and fired him. He had no choice. He gave him a chance. Then another. And another. I tried to tell him to keep it relaxed. Cut down on the drinking. He's like a kid in a candy store. He can't get enough of it."

Rossi nods. He understands. Eric, and they, witnessed Francis Martin's final impulsive act at Brewery Lane. It's better for everyone he moved on.

"I hope he doesn't think I had something to do with it," Eric says. "Ed wanted to know what happened. I said it was a disagreement. I didn't say anything about it getting nasty as it did. He heard that from someone else."

"Let's face it, it was bad," Rossi says.

Over the following weeks and months much of the news they hear about Francis Martin comes filtered through Eric. Someone saw him and he seemed happy. Someone else said they ran into him smoking outside a bar and he mentioned he had a delivery job for a beer distributer. Another said they talked to him and he was thinking of moving to Philly.

And that's where this story about Francis Martin should end, with his going off to a fresh start in a new city. But that kind of wrap up would be too easy a way out for him.

For a while the gossip about Francis Martin goes quiet. His name is mentioned less and less. A year goes by when Eric shares the bad news with them.

Francis Martin was out on a delivery when he got into a wreck on the Cross Bronx Expressway. He had to be rushed to a hospital. He had surgery on his jaw and an eye. He had several broken ribs. Still exposed to an abundance of the product, he was drinking that day.

Months after that Rossi reads the group text from Eric. Francis Martin was having a going away party at a bar near his place on Montrose Ave. His paintings would be for sale and soon after that he was moving back to Denver to be near his family.

"I don't know the specifics," Eric says when they're standing by the taps.

"We'll find out what's up when we're there," Rossi says.

"If he's going back to Colorado, it couldn't be good," Davis says.

"Not at all," Eric says with a slow shake of his head. He picks a glass off the shelf. "You guys going to order, or you just sightseeing?"

Pints in hand, Rossi and Davis tap glasses. Rossi proposes a toast. "To Father Francis, for wide is the gate and long is the road that leads to the destruction so many enter into."

Davis says, "To Brother Eric, may he not tread down that same path."

"May we all walk the one that avoids it," Eric says and starts to the register.

ABOUT THE LETTER

About the letter that arrived at my mother's apartment two months after my father's death addressed from a postal code in Ohio, I will say this, I wasn't surprised. It also wasn't a shock she never mentioned it and that it came to my attention by accident a year later when I was visiting her and discovered it in the grocery bag of notes and cards we, my mother, brother Peter and I received from relatives and friends wanting to express their condolences during our time of loss. So many kind words and thoughts even if many, most I'll add, seemed related to a fictitious two-dimensional character. Which I know was the identity my father preferred to exhibit to the world; a pliant, not very complicated man without much of an interior life.

Angela,

I am sorry this comes at such a late date. I hope it doesn't bother you to get it. I only heard last week Bill had passed away and I wanted to send you something. I know how difficult a time this must be for you and your boys. Bill was a good, dear man. It's too bad there aren't more like him in this life. I wish you peace and best of luck.

With warm regards,
Beverley Tapper

What had she thought of it? The question came and it wasn't in reference to the letter's author. Had my mother known about Beverly Tapper? Or about anything that went on with my father from the time after Peter and I were teenagers and the two of them separated in all ways but the rooms they ate and watched television in? The portion of life they shared was the point of an iceberg that could be seen bobbing above water.

On the couch, my mother gone to her room for the night, everything began to sway and veer in obedience to what was implied on the paper pressed between my fingers. I felt a sudden and strange reconnection to a Sunday morning in central New York state, when I traveled with my father to a regional archery tournament. And that was when I knew I'd met Beverley Tapper.

The tournament was the season's biggest and it created a stir in my father that had built up over several weeks. His mood brightened whenever he talked about it. At the time I hadn't yet reached the required skill level to get a tournament card for my age group, but my father let me go with him as if I had.

That year it was held in Watkins Glen, a town at the southern end of Lake Seneca. The drive from Worcester took much of the hot August afternoon that passed with the windows down and a breeze snapping my hair and sleeves of my jersey. It was dinner time when my father rolled to a stop at the motel he'd booked weeks earlier, a two-story strip of red brick with woods behind it. Each of the rooms had a plate-glass window and gray slab of metal serving as a door. We ate at the Jack-in-the-Box down the road. That was followed by a cup of ice cream bought at a shed that made its own. With an hour of light left, we went back to the motel and watched baseball. All the while I felt the excitement building in my father to an intensity that seemed unusual. Twice he went outside to use the payphone under the NO VACANCY sign. After his second time out there I wondered why he didn't use the one in the room?

"More expensive when you call from here," he answered to my satisfaction. "They take advantage of you if you're lazy."

He was gone fifteen minutes each time, not so long, and there didn't seem to be anything more to it.

In the morning he drove us to the range and parked in a dirt space between two other cars. He carried his bow. I took the quiver with a dozen aluminum arrows with orange-and-white feathers. The nervous energy I felt vibrating in him at the Registration Desk was that of an athlete before the start of a competition. A nervousness, I knew, that would settle down once the first target was engaged, the taut polyester string drawn back, the black bulls-eye locked in his squinting eyes.

My father asked the man behind the table for a ten o'clock start time and got it. The man returned a smile, glad he could satisfy my father's wishes.

"Bobby, you must be starving. Let's get you something to eat."

We turned away and headed to the carts and grills, where food was being cooked and served and the smell of sizzling meat started a sea of saliva foaming in my mouth. The can of sugary orange soda and bag of peanuts I'd bought from machines in the motel's office was all I'd had. My father only had coffee. But he didn't seem to be thinking of food as much as I was. His eyes were on the lookout for what must have been something more than food. A shooting partner, I supposed. Someone he was tight with. Someone he made the round of targets with on the weekends they could get to the same tournaments.

I brought the paper plate of scrambled eggs, fried potatoes and bacon over to the shade of an overhanging branch where my father was talking to a woman with light-brown hair and large eyes. She wore khaki pants and a short-sleeved green shirt that hung loose at her waist. An athletic looking woman. Around my mother's age. But unlike her I saw she had a casual manner and easy smile.

My father and this woman, he'd introduced her as Bev, seemed to meet up as if planned. The natural getting together of two people that liked each other. Even though it wasn't my mother, knowing women as well as men at a tournament that had divisions for both seemed without any other intent.

"You comfortable enough down there, Bobby? Looks like you settled right in."

Bev liked me. I knew by the way her eyes rolled over me, her concern if I had enough to eat?

"I'm okay right now, thanks," I answered and went back to my food.

My father and Bev went on talking as I stabbed gobs of egg and brought them to my mouth. The conversation I heard them having wasn't about the competition, as I'd expected. Instead, it was about them. My father and Bev. About what they did and how they felt since they last saw each other.

"Two more months gone just like that," Bev said.

"Time flies, and money goes fast," my father replied with a favorite saying of his.

From that they went on about their practice shoots back home and how they expected to do out on the course. Then my father mentioned his leg was bothering him, though he didn't think it would affect his score. It was a war injury, and it had been a long time since I heard him mention it, as if he'd banged it getting out of the motel's shower. No, it had been going on a couple of weeks. Once in a while he had to stop and wait for the pain to go away.

"They can't do anything?" Bev said. Her hand reached out and touched my father's arm.

"Nothing," my father said. "Been to every doctor at the V.A. They all tell me the same damn thing. We can give you pills. I don't want to take pills."

By the time I was done with my food a bearded man had joined them and the topic switched to the tournament.

"This wind could make things a whole lot tricky on the long targets," the man said.

Then the megaphone announcement was made. The rounds were about to start. My father gave me a few dollars, then he, Bev and the other man took their bows and quivers over to the clubhouse where the archers were gathering.

Back to that letter I kept for myself the night I was visiting my mother. I had forgotten, remembered, forgotten and rediscovered it this spring when I went looking for it a few weeks after she died at the age of eighty-one.

The postal code on the envelope led me to a town on the Ohio River named Epson. The occupant at 32 Walsh Street, a tree-lined street of single-family homes, three blocks from Epson's town square, I saw on Google Earth, is now seventy-nine years old. It was easy enough to get Beverley Tapper's phone number off the Internet. Last night I called her not sure if she'd remember me or want to talk. But Beverley Tapper hadn't forgotten. She didn't deny my natural desire to want to know about her and my father. To hear about that part of his life I never knew. In fact, after two hours it was at my insistence we ended when we did. We agreed to stay in touch by phone. "I'm not on Facebook, or any of them," she'd said.

After I hung up I went back over the two weeks my father took off by himself without any clear reason. The suspicions everyone had about where he went and why faded away until he took off again two years later and then a year after that. "Time outs," he'd called those. One more trip was made the following year and I was right to anticipate Beverley Tapper would be able to fill those gaps in.

There had been a visit to Ohio to stay with her. The next time they met up at the Grand Canyon and another time in Montreal. Their final get-together was spent in Mexico. After that, I don't recall my father going away by himself for any long stretches, though I'm not certain.

And then something Beverley Tapper said at the end of our conversation floated back to me as if an answer from a Magic Eight Ball: "I don't think I was the only one he was with like that, Robert."

The implication of that sentence opens up more questions so I'll leave it at that until after the next time I talk to her.

PROVENANCE

Every once in a while movers in dark jerseys, jeans and thick-soled shoes come to get me. They wrap me in plastic and bands of foam padding. Then they slide me into a wood crate that's a perfect fit, was made just for me. When I'm secure, they load me into the back of a truck and take me to the airport. Not long after that I'm in the air and on my way to Los Angeles, London, Sao Paulo and other exciting cities, where important people await my safe arrival.

Hanging in an exhibit that thousands come to each day, where I stand out even in the best company, is when I'm most happy. I'm admired for who and what I am, a masterful work of Vincent's, one of the last he made in that feverish burst of energy in Auvers when he was living with my namesake Dr. Gachet. Three days was all he needed to finish my poignant structure of lines, colors and forms that makes me one of the world's most famous paintings.

You may think I live a glamorous life. All the attention, travel, pictures taken and so many articles written about me. But it's not always that way. Any museum catalog can give you my basic facts: my height and width, the year of my creation, my provenance. But you'll read nothing of my internal life. From the moment Vincent finished me, still haunted by the tormenting spirits that would soon overwhelm him, I began to see being a great work of art isn't easy.

Like you, I've lived and learned. Like you, I've known disappointment and desperation. Feelings that began when Theo's wife Joanna showed me in public for the first time and I didn't sell. Snubbed by everyone, they preferred others to me. That was in Copenhagen, 1893. A long time ago, I know. But who doesn't remember their first rejection. That stab in the belly that strikes without warning. That makes you queasy and stays with you forever.

After that, Joanna stored me in a dark room with others by Vincent. Stunning yellow wheat fields. Violet, hallucinatory courtyards. An amiable postman. Like me, they were beautiful visions of Vincent's. I saw them when Joanna lit the oil lamp to show us to strangers. She became the executor of Vincent's paintings after Theo died. It was Joanna who collected their letters and sought to get them published. Without *Dear Theo* Vincent and I wouldn't be thought of as well as we are. We owe our fame to Joanna.

Four years went by before Ambroise Vollard, one of the most important art dealers in Europe, bought me. That was in 1897. When he picked me out I knew my fortunes would change. And they did, but not the way I expected.

Right away Vollard put me in a group exhibit in Paris. A fine one too. Well attended and publicized. That was where Alice Ruben, a beautiful woman with dark eyes and long brown hair, spotted me next to one of Gauguin's Tahitian paintings. While I'm not as exotic as a bare-breasted native woman holding a crude wooden bowl with mangoes in it, I'm deep, true, honest and open with my feelings. That was why Alice favored me. Why she bought me from Vollard for an amount that gave him a large profit. Even so, I was happy to go to a fine home in Copenhagen occupied by a sensitive, intelligent woman.

While I knew Alice loved me, she loved many things and she had many things to love. There's a photo of her taken with me when she was pregnant. She's filled with life, a few months from becoming a mother for the first time. A full smile fills her face that induces one of your own. There's no evidence she intended to transfer ownership of me to the art dealer Mogens Ballin a month after it was taken. I was with her for less than a year.

It goes without saying I wasn't happy with Ballin. He was an insensitive man who kept me locked in a lightless room for seven years. To him I was an object to hold onto until my value went up instead of one of intrinsic beauty and profound depth, with feelings and a soul that aches to be wanted. Did Vincent in his maddened state foresee that? Is that the reason he gave me, as that perceptive critic described, the heartbroken expression of our time?

In 1904 Ballin sold me to Harry Kessler, though I'd wanted to go with the gray-haired lady Mrs. Land. Three times Mrs. Land came to see me. Three times I was set out on a dusty table for her to look at.

She was a warm woman. It was a joy to be the object of her gaze. Each time she went to Ballin's she stayed longer, her thoughtful eyes taking all of me in. The last time she visited she pleaded with Ballin to lower his price. There was something about the angle of my head resting in my hand that touched her. The books on the table next to me did too. She loved to read, she told him. But it was my melancholic appearance that reflects my sorrow for the human condition and not my own troubles as everyone thinks that attracted Mrs. Land. I could tell it was how she felt too. At the end of the day I didn't go home with her.

For four years I hung in Harry Kessler's Berlin home, fourteen of the finest, most opulently decorated rooms you'll ever see. I had impressive company on the walls around me: Cezannes, Matisses and Renoirs. I was the only painting by Vincent that Harry owned. In truth he didn't like Vincent much. He thought him a crude sensibility. But he wanted to tell his friends and associates he owned one. That was the reason he took me from Ballin. Otherwise, he favored Cezanne's cold cylindrical abstractions and Matisse's decorative patterns I much prefer over Cezanne. Then, after a few years, he gave up on me just as Alice had. He didn't want me for the reasons Mrs. Land did. Most who've desired me for more than my value couldn't afford me. Those who could didn't keep me around long. Plenty of others were available to them.

In 1911 the museum director Georg Swarzenski purchased me from a gallery in Paris for the new Stadelsches Kunstinstitute in Frankfort. I was proud to be one of the museum's main acquisitions. In Swarzenski's learned opinion I was an example of artistic experience transmitted in as perfect and direct a way as was possible. A work of great profundity and true substance. I wanted to stay there forever.

That was a glorious time in my life. Vincent was becoming famous, as was I. Those who loved art identified with the honesty he expressed in his paintings. They felt the struggle and tension of his life in them. They must have seen in him, in me, their own difficulties exposed.

For twenty years I was secure with my place in the world. I thought it would last forever. But nothing does. Comfort's illusory. Political stability is too. The climate in Germany changed. People were angry at unseen forces that complicated their lives. They were incited by a single man to do something about it. My friends and I in the Stadelsches Kunstinstitute feared the evil lurking about us. For good reason. The unseen forces stepped out of the shadows. At the Fuhrer's request Joseph Goebbels took control of the visual arts. The Fuhrer believed modern art was decadent. That Vincent belonged to a long line of depraved artists and was a danger to the German people's morale. On his orders I was taken down and locked away. In that room I dreaded each approaching footstep. I never stopped worrying I would be harmed.

When the war began in 1938 Franz Koeings, a courageous man, a lover of art, of Vincent, of me, negotiated for my release. It wasn't easy. It took many months to convince Goebbels I should be rescued from oblivion. Those negotiations were done in secret. As was my escape. Late one night Franz rolled me up, shut me in a suitcase and snuck me across the border. In Amsterdam I was relieved to no longer be thought of as a pathetic example of cultural Bolshevism and included in exhibitions themed "degenerate art."

Soon I had a private owner, a stern, ambitious gentleman from the United States.

Seigfried Kramarsky brought me to his duplex on New York's West Side. A curving staircase connected the two floors with glorious views over Central Park's treetops. I shared a large, bright room with a delicate interior design with paintings much older than me. Nevertheless, they were impressive. A self-portrait by Rembrandt. A Franz Hals. A Piero della Francesca. It was a comfortable life for us. I was treated with respect. Well taken care of, though I desired to go back to a museum where I'd be appreciated by more than friends and guests.

When Mr. Kramarsky died I'd hoped that would happen. A year earlier Vincent's vases of sunflowers and another of irises brought tens of millions. Knowing that, his daughter Sonja put me up for auction at Sotheby's.

Right away there was speculation I would become the highest priced painting ever sold. I was locked in a vault until the bidding started. Once it did, it took just minutes for me to break the record. When the final number was called out, I was valued at eighty-two million dollars. Overnight fame came to me just like that. My photo was reproduced on the front page of newspapers around the world. Yet I continued to despair. The look in my eyes hadn't changed. No museum could afford me. Only an international bank. Three days later I was flown to Tokyo and put up in a special room where I was gawked at for my celebrity, my value as a commodity. That was what my existence had come down to.

Fame comes and goes. Money does too.

The next year Asian currencies collapsed. Economies followed. The bank that purchased me was in trouble. I was transferred like valueless securities back to Sotheby's, where I now spend my days in a subbasement like an old piece of furniture that can't be sold. In storage, wrapped in cotton inside a box, owned but not loved, I yearn to give myself to others, to everyone who wants to look at me. Isn't that what art's for? To be shared? But here I am, left to the whims of my owners and the state of the market, that speculative and despicable exchange that makes a few want to spend millions on me then store me in the dark. They feel nothing for me. Nor for those wanting to see me.

I'm all alone. I don't get out much. I sit and wait. But for what? This must be the reason Vincent gave me the sad expression he did. Why he propped my head up on one elbow as if to show my submission to the fate that greater forces had in store for me. Did he anticipate I would suffer as he did? Only for longer. For much, much longer.

A NICE PLACE TO LIVE

Twenty years before the real estate boom we bought our place from the lady who lived across the street. Her name was Mary, and while she had plenty of other offers, she'd taken a liking to us.

"You mean she liked you more than me," Lucy said.

Maybe that was true. No, it *was* true. More than once Mary mentioned I reminded her of her dead husband Louis even if I didn't see much of a resemblance. Louis was a lifelong iron worker. I'm a cubicle jockey for a company downtown. Louis had a high school degree. I have a graduate degree. Louis was rugged. Me, not so much of that. But I wasn't about to tell Mary what to think.

Anyway, Mary was seventy-six at the time she decided to go live upstate with her daughter. It just so happened that after seven years renting a one bedroom across the street we were looking to buy a home of our own. The problem was, there weren't many places in our price range that didn't need an expensive rehab we didn't have the extra money for.

Now I don't want to sound insensitive, but it was our good fortune Mary's brother-in-law Henry died just as we were wondering if we'd be able to stay in the neighborhood, close to friends and interests. Henry lived on the first floor and Mary had been looking after him. When George from down the street, George's ears were like radio dishes when it came to local gossip, when he told us Mary was selling, our hopes rose. We knew we had to go see her.

Two evenings later Mary met us at her door in a printed house dress. Her gray hair was tied up in a bun. On the second floor she made us tea and Lucy and I sat with her at the kitchen table, an old-school type of table with a green formica top and chairs that matched.

We told Mary how sorry we were Henry was gone. How concerned we'd been when we didn't see him sitting out on the front porch.

"He always said he wanted to go quick, and that's what happened," Mary said. She appeared pleased to know Henry didn't suffer much.

Henry took up a lot of the conversation in that hour. Though there was still enough time left for Mary to go off about how much the neighborhood had changed. In her opinion, it wasn't for the better for older people like her. Though it was still a nice block to live on, she wasn't saying that.

"If I was your age again I'd want to stay here too," she said. "But I can't afford to take care of all this. I'd have to get a tenant and that would be more of a pain for me."

After that we told Mary how her place was just right for us. That we wanted to buy it from her.

She was happy to hear we were interested. I think she liked the idea of passing it on to people she knew would appreciate it.

"We're not going to flip it, or just sit on it, do nothing and wait for the price to go up," I said.

"We want to live in it and enjoy it," Lucy said.

"Louis thought a lot of you." Mary looked at me. "He always said you were a nice couple to have as neighbors."

We left with Mary's promise to sell us the place, but she'd have to talk to her children before it was official. The next morning I got a call from her daughter. She said the house was ours as long as we matched the highest bid.

Needless to say, three months later we went to the offices of Mary's lawyer to close on it. Needless to say, it still cost us a pretty penny to get the apartments in the shape we wanted. As with all old houses, there were surprises in store. Mold, leaks, faulty wiring and a few other matters Mary either didn't know about or had ignored for years.

"As many as twenty," the electrician told us.

Those first weeks we talked a lot about how much owning a piece of property had bettered our lives. We were no longer captives to a neglectful owner like the one we had across the street. There would be no more bugs, mice, or repairs taken care of only when a disaster struck; a burst pipe flooding a room or an old appliance that kept breaking down. We make it a point to treat our property right. We try to treat our tenants right too. We don't charge outrageous rent. We're trusting, we don't need them to sign a lease every year. We're not suckers, but we prefer to make it worth their while to stay and worth our while to have them around. If they need something done, we take care of it. We do our best to make it a nice place to live.

Which I guess is why all these years later we've only had three different sets of renters on the first floor.

Alice and Martha stayed for eleven years and they're still our favorites. A fine couple. So quiet, we never knew if they were home or away. Never a complaint about anything. To say the least, we were sorry to see them go. Though happy they were able to buy a condo in a new development down the block and we get to socialize with them now and then.

The next couple lasted three years. Simon and Rosa were young, not married when they moved in. Then they got hitched, had a baby and needed more room. We understood. They moved to a bigger place over in Queens and we wished them well.

The most recent, Pete and Dorothy, have a consulting business that takes them out of town a lot. Strategy consulting for media, according to their website. They're always heading off somewhere. We never know just where that is. They don't tell us much and we don't ask questions. The lease we all signed didn't mention anything about having to get know each other. They have their quirks, as we all do. I'll give you one example, they shop online for everything. I mean everything. No two days go by there isn't a package or three waiting for them outside the front door that we end up taking into the hallway. That sit there until they're back from wherever they were at.

Of course, we weren't concerned when they went away for an entire month. It'd happened before. They have a business to run that takes them here and there. We get it. We're not complaining. The place is all ours when they're away and Lucy and I need some of that.

When they didn't come back a second month we wondered if everything was all right? If there was an emergency? An ill parent maybe?

By then we figured it wasn't out of bounds to want to know that much. Lucy sent an email asking what was up? Was there anything we could do for them?

The thing was, no reply came back. No word about what they were up to. Or about sending rent. Which didn't worry us too much. Every month they dropped a check in our mailbox on the 1st. Like clockwork, it was waiting there in the morning. Not this time, but we figured everyone needs a little space to be forgetful.

Then there were the packages piling up in the hallway. Five, ten, then fourteen, I counted. Big and small boxes and mailers, a lot with foreign addresses that got us wondering what was in them? They might not be around, but stuff kept arriving. Enough so we had to squeeze past it all to get to the basement door.

When another two weeks went by, another unanswered email from Lucy saying we needed to hear from them soon, we'd just about had it.

"It's getting weird," I said.

"They could at least send a few words back," Lucy said.

The situation was staring us in the face every day. No rent. Packages stacking up. Lucy was walking around muttering to herself. I was doing likewise. We'd hoped to never get to this point, in a predicament with our tenants. We'd seen *Pacific Heights*. We'd read the horror stories online about people walking away and leaving everything they owned behind.

It was a touchy situation taking over our lives. Every day we were losing money. Every day we had to look at those packages. Every day we were getting more frustrated. And yet, what could we do? Wait for them to come back all apologetic? Were they coming back at all?

Two weeks later I told Lucy, "It's three months. Time to wave bye bye and get someone else in here."

"It's way past that time," she said. Her face was squeezed tight, as it gets when something irritates her.

The next day we went down the street to meet with Alice, our lawyer. Sitting across her big wood desk, Alice assured us since there was no current lease they were tenants at will, meaning we were within our legal right to evict them. Before that happened, she'd try to locate them online to see if she could find out what they were up to.

"Who cares," I told her. The voice I said it in was louder than my usual voice. I lowered it a bit, "It's all right to go into their place without their permission? We need to know what's going on."

It was, Alice said. We owned it after all, even if we were starting to feel it was the other way around. I mean, who knew what kind of condition they left it in?

"Do we have to notify any authority?" Lucy said.

"No, legally they've surrendered the apartment back to you," Alice said.

The next day we were a little on edge. What homeowner wouldn't be? Almost a year had gone by since we were in there to check out a problem.

Keying the lock, we held our breath. We didn't know what we'd find. We relaxed when we saw nothing was rotting out in the open, no bugs were scooting around the sinks or tub, that dust kitties were the worst of it. The air was stale, but overall the place was in okay shape. We did notice the packages we'd carried into the hallway all those years had brought a lot of top-quality items: a fancy espresso maker, lamps, candelabra, pots and pans, exotic framed photos. Even their vacuum cleaner was choice.

Later that morning Alice called us. She couldn't find them anywhere.

I wondered, "You think they're in witness protection? Or they're spies? I never felt the names Pete and Dorothy were a good match for their faces. It was like they didn't grow into them."

Alice laughed, even if I wasn't trying to be funny. What were the possibilities? Did Alice know something she was prohibited from telling us?

"Are they still alive?" I said.

"I can't give you an answer to that," she said. "Their site's still up, but it hasn't been updated of late. There's no trail to follow from there."

"We need to get everything out and the place cleaned up and rented. We need to know what to do with their stuff. No way we're gonna pay to store it."

"That's up to you now," she said. "If anyone tells you otherwise, have them give me a call."

There was no one to wrangle with about what to do with their belongings. After a bit of discussion, Lucy and I decided on something we'd never done, and it was her idea: "Let's have a stoop sale. Everyone else has them, why not us?"

We had a laugh. We couldn't help it. Whatever money we made we'd add to the security deposit to use as payment for the unpaid rent. Anything we didn't sell we'd donate to charity.

After Lucy said that we realized the packages had to be opened and we'd need to do the same with whatever was in them.

"Or, if it's any good we keep it," I said.

"I like that better." Lucy smiled.

Tearing them open, we felt like kids at Christmas. We got ourselves a rice cooker shipped from Thailand. A quilt from India. A couple of casual men's shirts from Turkey that fit me just fine. The smallest box had a Mont Blanc pen with two refills that Lucy claimed for herself. That came from Switzerland.

"They did like to order their things from the source," Lucy said.

"I do like that they did," I said.

That Saturday and Sunday we carried a good amount of their stuff out the door and had that stoop sale. We took in five hundred for the bikes alone.

"They were pricey, we could have got more," Lucy said.

When it was over, we'd brought in over a month of rent. We also got a tax deduction for gifting a couch, tables and other items to Sally Ann's. We ended up making something from a situation we expected to take a bath on. We were feeling a lot better about it.

The next week Meagan over at G.P. Properties hooked us up with a nice couple. He was a barista. She worked in interior design. They were excited to have a new home and we were looking forward to them moving in the beginning of the month.

"See, it turned out just fine," I told Lucy one evening in the kitchen.

She poured us glasses of wine and we tapped them together. "All's good now," she said.

We went into the living room. I sat on the couch and clicked around the stations to see what was on television. Lucy went to the computer. She was there a few minutes when she screamed: *"No. No way. Come look at this. No way."*

I went over to see what it was that startled her.

Pete and Dorothy were out of the country on a dream trip they'd planned for years. They almost never checked that email account and assumed we knew that. They were sorry for any trouble they might have caused us. They just found out their bank hadn't released the rent checks due to an authorization glitch. The funds would be expressed to us the next day. They themselves would be back in a week.

HOPE THE PACKAGES AREN'T TOO MUCH OF A BOTHER

WE LOVE LIVING THERE

YOUR TENANTS, PETE & DOROTHY

www.ingramcontent.com/pod-product-compliance
Lightning Source LLC
Chambersburg PA
CBHW020854160726
47993CB00004B/1660